A–Z
OF
STOCKPORT
PLACES - PEOPLE - HISTORY

Robert Nicholls

AMBERLEY

First published 2021

Amberley Publishing
The Hill, Stroud, Gloucestershire, GL5 4EP
www.amberley-books.com

Copyright © Robert Nicholls, 2021

The right of Robert Nicholls to be identified as
the Author of this work has been asserted in
accordance with the Copyrights, Designs and
Patents Act 1988.

ISBN 978 1 4456 9308 8 (print)
ISBN 978 1 4456 9309 5 (ebook)

British Library Cataloguing in Publication Data.
A catalogue record for this book is available
from the British Library.

Typesetting by SJmagic DESIGN SERVICES,
India. Printed in Great Britain.

Contents

Introduction

Writing a book about Stockport presents challenges. It is a town with a long history stretching back to the Middle Ages, but whose identity has in more recent times due to urban growth become entwined with its larger neighbour, Manchester, only 7 miles away, town centre to city centre. This makes for a town of contrasts, and in my view is one of the reasons why Stockport is such an interesting place.

Geographically, there is a relatively flat west, now mainly covered with housing, and a hilly eastern fringe, with its mixture of farms and extended villages that have their origins in the decades of the Industrial Revolution, and which today make for an interesting townscape and provide historical interest.

All is divided by the westerly-flowing River Mersey, arising in the town centre at the confluence of the rivers Goyt and Etherow. The rivers also provide the historical boundary between Lancashire and Cheshire. And yes, Stockport, in both its pre- and post-1974 local authority forms, was partly in Lancashire, although few realise this. The majority however is in Cheshire – another reason for the contrasts evident in the town.

Buildings and locations of historical and local interest exist all over the town. In the north is the nineteenth-century village of Reddish, with its housing, existing mills and a Waterhouse-designed church. The town centre around the market is very attractive and merits greater visitor interest. There are a number of notable churches and good museums reflecting matters from the town's past, including hat-making, the Air-raid Shelters and Bramall Hall. They tend to be small in nature, but Stockport does them well; the town wisely lets its larger neighbour provide the larger attractions. And then, as an exception to this rule, there is a great stately home of Lyme Hall and Park, just outside the present-day borough boundaries but sufficiently connected with the town to merit inclusion in this book, and one of the National Trust's most visited properties.

The eastern fringes of the borough provide lots of visual and historic interest, with the Peak Forest and Macclesfield canals stretching through Romiley, Marple and High Lane, the attractive village of Compstall and the Etherow and Chadkirk Country Parks.

Stockport has produced many notable inhabitants. Many have become figures of national importance. From the past we have one of the 'Cockleshell Heroes', the man who helped discover the North West Passage, the pioneer of the first stored-programme computer, a noted mountaineer, several suffragettes and the first successful British tennis player, whose name lives on in a well-known brand of sportswear.

Because of the proximity of television stations in nearby Manchester, and the music industry in that city, Stockport's contribution to the worlds of media, performance and music could well be greater that other towns of similar size. Joan Bakewell, Michelle Keegan, Claire Foy, Mike Yarwood, David Dickinson are to name but a few.

When I was first embarking on this project, a friend rather disparagingly asked me how I was going to make Stockport interesting? He had not given any thought to a town he knew so well. Having lived in the town in the past for several decades, this task has not been difficult for me, and I hope that those who read this book will come to the same conclusion.

A

Abney Hall

Agatha Christie often visited Abney Hall, as the last private owner, the grandson of Sir James Watts, was the author's brother-in-law. The novel *After the Funeral* and the short story *The Adventure of the Christmas Pudding* were both written from there. The house was also the inspiration for 'Chimneys', the fictional country seat of the Marchioness of Caterham, as well as a number of other country houses which were woven into the author's plots. Queen Victoria's husband, Prince Albert, and King Edward VII also visited.

The building occupies the site of the former Cheadle Grove Print Works, which stood here from 1760 until destroyed by fire. The hall was built between 1842 and 1847 and was at first the home of the Mayor of Stockport and cotton magnate Alfred Orell. It was originally called 'The Grove' after the former printworks.

Orell died in the year of its completion and it was sold to Manchester textile magnate James Watts, who undertook alterations and extensions in the early 1850s. The architects were the same as those who designed the former Watts Warehouse,

Abney Hall southern elevation viewed from the park.

now the Britannia Hotel on Portland Street in Manchester. Soon after the completion of these works, Watts engaged the famous architect A. W. N. Pugin to make further alterations.

Watts renamed the building Abney Hall after Sir Walter Abney, who 'entertained Isaac Watts, for over 30 years'. Further alterations took place in the 1890s.

In 1958 it was bought by the former Cheadle and Gatley Urban District Council for use as a town hall, and it was inherited by Stockport Council in 1974, after which most of the hall's remaining historical furniture was moved to other historic houses controlled by the council. Much of the surrounding land was also sold for development. The hall is now privately owned and is used as offices, but the remaining park land is open to the public. Tours of the hall are sometimes available on Heritage Open Days each September.

Air Raid Shelters

Stockport's extensive air-raid shelter system was excavated in the soft sandstone by the local authority in the months following the Munich crisis of September 1938, and became one of the few large shelter systems to be provided outside London. Three separate systems were excavated: at Brinksway, Dodge Hill, and Chestergate on the south side of the town centre. The latter were the largest and were built as extensions to existing shallow caves. The total capacity was for 6,500 and there is almost a mile of tunnels.

The shelters were equipped with electricity, wooden seating, steel beds (of which many remain in situ today), toilets (both water and chemical) and a first-aid post. They saw extensive use during the Second World War, being referred to locally at one

Stockport Air Raid Shelters, entrance on Chestergate.

time as the 'Chestergate Hilton', and many residents of Manchester also travelled out by tram to use them. Towards the end of the war they were closed and largely forgotten.

During the 1980s ideas began to emerge about opening the Chestergate site up for tourism, and in 1990 Stockport Museum began running guided tours through them. Part of the system has since been re-equipped as it would have been during the war, and visitors can now wander around these areas. Guided 'Explorer' tours (with miners' helmets and lamps) are also available in the undeveloped rear parts, which have been left as they were at the end of the war to provide (as one guidebook says) 'a dark and forbidding reminder of the suffering caused by war, as well as a tribute to the ingenuity and the will to survive of an earlier generation'.

All Saints' Church, Marple

The present church on this site dates from 1880, having replaced an earlier church dating from 1811 which had become too small for its congregation. The tower of the older building however remains, detached from the present-day church, and contains, internally, memorials to the Revd Kelsall Prescott (who died in 1828), to Samuel Oldknow (see later entry) by the noted sculptor Francis Chantrey, Elizabeth Isherwood, Nathaniel Wright and John Clayton. The tower also holds eight bells.

At one corner of the churchyard is a stable and coach house built for the use of the owner of Marple Hall when attending church, and a hearse house adjoining. Country areas had the use of what was effectively a 'village hearse' for use in times of bereavement, particularly for the paupers of the parish. It was usually a long black cart decorated with black plumes at each corner and pulled by a horse supplied by

View of the current All Saints' Church, Marple.

Left: The isolated tower of the 1811 church.

Below: The hearse house and the Lord of the Manor's carriage building, All Saints' Church.

a local farmer. The hearse would be kept in such a building, as here, provided by the parish authorities. Hearse houses fell out of use in the later nineteenth century when firms of undertakers became commonplace. Both buildings date from the early nineteenth century.

Today, All Saints' is very much a church in the evangelical tradition. Marple's other Anglican church, St Martin's near Marple Bridge, is more Anglo-Catholic, and is often referred to as 'the high church in Low Marple'.

Arden Hall

This house, now a ruin, was once the home of one of Stockport's most notable families, the Arderns (sometimes spelt Ardens or Ardernes). A wattle and daub hall had existed on the site since 1331, being rebuilt in 1597, the date appearing on the right-hand gable (along with the initials R A) and on a spout above the entrance.

The family also owned Great Underbank Hall in the town centre (see elsewhere in this book) and more substantial estates in the Midlands, where there is a connection to William Shakespeare.

Surrounded by a moat and sitting on a commanding site overlooking the River Tame, the building was reputedly used to house Parliamentarians during the Civil War during the Siege of Manchester, although apart from the name of the access road, Battle Lane, there is no real evidence of this.

The house was modernised and a new stable block constructed in 1728–34, but the family ceased to use it circa 1795. Thereafter it was partly used as a farmhouse, and after the death of the last male heir in 1850 it was sold to pay off gambling debts. By 1866 it had lost its roof and some of the walls had collapsed. Two modern dwellings have been constructed from the remains of some of the nearby outbuildings. Close access is not possible without prior permission.

Arden Hall, Bredbury, frontage view.

B

Back, George

Arctic explorer Admiral George Back was born in Stockport in 1796 and was educated at Stockport Grammar School. He joined the Royal Navy as a volunteer in 1808 and during action in the Bay of Biscay the following year, he was captured by the French and held prisoner until 1814.

By 1818, he had volunteered to take part on one of John Franklin's Arctic expeditions, including overland explorations, where he took responsibility for surveying and map-making. By 1825, he had been made a Commander, although he was technically unemployed from 1827 to 1833. In the latter year, he set out and led another expedition to find the explorer John Ross, missing since 1829, taking a route northwards to find and follow the Great Fish River. This he did, until he reached the Arctic Ocean. He then turned back and reached home in 1835. Ross, in the meantime, had reached England. The river, never before seen by a white man, was subsequently renamed Back's Fish River, and later still the Back River.

Admiral George Back. Those who wish to know more about Back are advised to consult an excellent booklet produced by the Stockport Heritage Trust.

A further expedition to the Frozen Strait followed in 1836–37, during which his ship the *Terror* was ice-bound for ten months, which caused damage. In a very poor condition, the *Terror* crossed the Atlantic reaching the coast of north-west Ireland, where it was beached near Lough Swilly.

Back was knighted in 1839. Due to poor health he retired from active service, although he remained on the Admiralty's books, becoming a rear-admiral in 1857, a vice-admiral in 1863 and finally an admiral in 1876. He died in 1878 and is buried in Kensal Green Cemetery in London.

Back was also an accomplished artist, writer and naturalist. Many of his paintings feature scenes from the Arctic and his expeditions.

Bakers Vaults

This is one of Stockport's most notable public houses, being located in Market Place. It has had the current name since 1861 when it was rebuilt to create additional space for the new Market Hall then being built. It was named after Charles Baker, one-time mayor of the town, who had run the previous pub on the site, called the George

Bakers Vaults in the Market Place.

and Dragon, from 1824. That pub had been built around 1775 on the foundations of Stockport's one-time castle.

Bakers Vaults is a Grade II listed building and is an excellent example of a Victorian 'Gin Palace'. For many years, it has been a live music venue. It was substantially refurbished in 2014.

Bakewell, Joan

Joan Bakewell (now Dame) was born Joan Dawson Rowlands in Heaton Moor in 1933. At an early date, the family moved to Hazel Grove and Joan attended Stockport High School for Girls – a state grammar school of the time, subsequently merged with another school to form the present-day Priestnall School. Her education progressed to Cambridge where she studied Economics and later History.

Bakewell has had a glittering career in television and journalism. First coming into public view on the BBC2 programme *Late Night Line-up* in the late 1960s, she expanded her career to include documentary and arts programmes, political debates, morality and quasi-religious presentations. She herself is a humanist and from 2017, after her elevation to the peerage in 2010, she has chaired the All-Party Humanist Group. She sits as a Labour peer. More recently, she has ventured into authorship.

Early in her television career, she was dubbed 'the thinking man's crumpet' by the television panellist and presenter the late Frank Muir. She is reported to dislike this description of her, but in the public view it remains.

Joan Bakewell arriving for the Women in Film and Television event at the Hilton Hotel, Park Lane, London, 2 December 2011. (Steve Vas/Featureflash/Shutterstock)

Bear Pit

Yes, Stockport had a bear pit and bear-baiting with dogs was carried out on this site until the practice was outlawed in 1835. Prizes were awarded to the best dogs who could pin the bear by its nose. Unlike cock-fighting, the bear was never killed. The man looking after the bear was usually called a 'bearward'. In some cases the bear was tethered; in others it had free run of a bear pit.

Nearby caves cut into the sandstone at the foot of High Bank Side were the places the bears were normally housed. A street above Chestergate was named Bearhole Brow.

The bear pit was partially re-created here in 1935 as part of the Mersey Square Improvements; its formal opening on 5 May 1935 is commemorated on a plaque attached to the rear wall. Flights of steps ran down to a paved area in the middle of which was a circular flower bed. However, the weight of the structure was beginning to cause damage to the arches over the river below, so in 2015 the area acquired its current circular form and the flower bed is no more. However, one of the town's main Christmas trees is placed here every December and in 2017 many mementoes were left here in memory of the twenty-two people killed in the Manchester Arena bombing, one of whom came from Stockport.

Bear Pit, with the A6 on the left-hand side and Mersey Square to the right.

Boardman, Peter

Peter Boardman was an outstanding mountaineer and author. Born in the town in 1950, he attended Stockport Grammar School from 1956 to 1969.

He started his climbing career in the nearby Peak District and whilst attending Nottingham University he spent a year as president of their mountaineering club.

After university he became an instructor in Aviemore, then the National Officer of the British Mountaineering Council, and from 1978 Director of the International School of Mountaineering in Switzerland.

Early climbs in Europe were followed by expeditions to the Hindu Kush, Alaska, Everest, Changabang in India, K2 and other sites in the Himalayas. His final expedition, to the north-east ridge of Everest, took place in 1982, where he was accompanied by Chris Tasker, Chris Bonington and others. During this climb, both Tasker and Boardman met their deaths, although it would be several years before Boardman's body would be discovered. A memorial service for him was held at St George's Church on 11 July 1982.

A Peter Boardman Climbing Wall was dedicated at Stockport Grammar School in 2008. Another such wall opened at Nottingham University in 2016.

Bramall Hall

This is one of the most prestigious buildings in the borough. It is a Grade I listed building. Note the difference in spelling between the name of the hall and those of its surrounding park and area in which it is located, both of which have an 'h'.

The oldest parts of the timber-framed building date from the fourteenth century. Through marriage in 1370 between Alice de Bromhale and John de Davenport, the latter family acquired the manor and following this it is likely that the first parts of the house were built. During the ownership of the fifth William Davenport after 1585, the hall was updated, including the addition of a long gallery, one of the 'status symbols' of any Tudor-era house.

By the early nineteenth century, the hall had passed to Salusbury Pryce Humphreys, the husband of the tenth William Davenport's illegitimate daughter, Maria. Disputes followed from other members of the Davenport family who claimed ownership. In 1838, Humphreys changed his name to Davenport. In 1869, the property was let to Wakefield Christy of one of the town's hat manufacturing companies. After a brief reoccupation by a member of the Davenport family, in 1877 the whole estate, then totalling 1,918 acres including the hall, was sold to the Manchester Freeholders Company for development purposes. After lying empty, in 1882 the hall was bought by Thomas Nevill, whose son, Charles, undertook substantial restoration and remodelling. Charles's nephew and adopted son, Thomas, inherited the estate in 1916 and in 1923 much of the furniture was sold at auction. An attempt to sell the house by auction failed, but a later private sale took place to John Davies, the president of Manchester United Football Club. After the death of his widow in 1935 it was bought by the local authority, then Hazel Grove and Bramhall Urban District Council. Since 1974, the house has been under the control of Stockport Metropolitan Borough.

Both hall and park are open to the public and are well worth visiting. Guided tours of the hall are available; alternatively, visitors can wander through on their own. Highlights of the interior include the Great Hall and the chapel, the latter being restored in the 1930s.

The hall has been used in many television productions, one of the more recent being as the fictional 'Southowram Hall' in the series *Last Tango in Halifax*.

Bramall Hall
western elevation.

Bramall Hall
eastern elevation.

C

Chadkirk Chapel

This small chapel, somewhat hidden away in a pleasant location in the Chadkirk Country Estate, owes its origins, it is said, to a religious oratory established on the site by Saint Chad, Bishop of Lichfield, AD 669–762. It is thought that there were never more than two monks based here.

There are mentions of a chapel here in 1347, and by the sixteenth century it had the status of a 'Chantry Chapel', where masses for the dead were said.

At the time of the Dissolution of the Monasteries it was claimed as a family chapel by the Davenports of Henbury, but the claim was disputed and the chapel was seized by the Crown. Later it was restored to the Davenports, following which it fell out of use.

By the 1640s it was being used by Puritan dissenters, and in 1689 it was formally registered as a nonconformist place of worship. The nonconformists were evicted in 1705, and again a period of disuse followed.

After falling into a ruinous condition it was restored by public subscription in 1747, from which date it served as Romiley's parish church until 1866. It was restored again in 1761, in 1860 and 1876. In 1971, after being used only for occasional Sunday

Chadkirk Chapel.

The walled garden at Chadkirk Chapel.

afternoon services for some time, it was declared redundant and sold to the local authority when the adjoining Country Estate was being first developed. Further restoration followed in 1973, and again in 1993–34. It is now open to the public on a regular basis at weekends, and wedding ceremonies can be conducted here.

The earliest parts of the building date from the Elizabethan time, but other sections are Georgian. The bell is inscribed '1750, God be with us all'.

The remainder of the Chadkirk Country Estate is well worth exploring. Close to the chapel is a walled garden, first laid out in 1745 by the Nicholson family who owned the estate and lived in the nearby house. The garden was restored in 2005.

Cheadle Hulme School

This is Stockport's other major private school, although neither it nor Stockport Grammar School are 'public' schools, as their present status dates from 1976 when the former Direct Grant system was abolished by Government.

Cheadle Hulme School's formal title is 'The Manchester Warehousemen and Clerks Orphan School', and this reflects the school's original foundation aims. A committee was formed in 1854 and established a set of rules as to how the school should be run together with admissions, which was to be for orphans and necessitous children of warehousemen and clerks only.

The school itself was founded in October 1855, but the committee had no premises, so the first children were sent to another school at Shaw Hall, Flixton, where boarding was possible. In 1861, the school moved to its own premises in Park Place, Ardwick in Manchester. The year 1867 saw work start on a purpose-built building on the present site, which opened in 1869. It is an extensive site, pleasantly wooded in places.

Cheadle Hulme School main elevation. (Cheadle Hulme School)

The school for a long period of its history included boarders, but from 1862 had accepted fee-paying boarders and day pupils to support the basic work of supporting orphaned and necessitous children. That policy remains embedded in the school today.

The school joined the Direct Grant Scheme in the mid-1920s and the school enjoyed a long period under the headship of T. R. Lockhart from then until the mid-1950s. Since then, further facilities have been added, including both Junior and Infant departments.

The school has always been fully co-educational. Boarding continued until the early 1990s. The school's motto is 'In loco parentis' – 'In place of the parent', and past pupils are known as 'Old Waconians' or 'Old Wacs'.

Cobden's Statue

Until the James Conway memorial was erected (see next entry), this was Stockport's only statue in the town centre, being located in St Peter's Square next to St Peter's Church.

Richard Cobden was the town's MP from 1841 to 1847. A founder member of the Anti-Corn Law League, he campaigned against the Corn Laws, which were a series of tariffs and trade restrictions on imported food and grain which helped to keep the price of bread high and led to starvation among the poor. They were finally repealed in 1846.

Above left: Richard Cobden statue in St Peter's Square.

Above right: Memorial to James Conway, 'Cockleshell Hero'.

Conway, James

This memorial, erected in 2017 on the site of the former Mount Tabor Methodist Chapel (see separate entry), commemorates James Conway, one of the 'Cockleshell Heroes' of the Second World War.

Conway, born in 1922, lived in Edgeley and was a milkman. He was one of twelve Royal Marines chosen to paddle by night over 80 miles up the River Gironde in canoes to plant mines on vessels in the port of Bordeaux, in western France, believed to be carrying materials for the German war effort.

They undertook four months of training near Portsmouth and what they were to do, codenamed 'Operation Frankton', was then revealed to them. The mission set off by submarine on 7 December 1942.

Some men drowned and others were captured and executed; only two members made it to the port, causing damage to six ships, most of which were quickly repaired. Lord Louis Mountbatten described it as the 'most courageous commando raid of the war' and Churchill is reported to have said that it shortened the war by six months. Conway, along with his colleague Lt John Mackinnon, were forced to abandon their canoe *Cuttlefish* after it was damaged several days into the raid. Both men made it ashore, but were captured and subsequently executed.

The attack was later depicted in the 1955 film *Cockleshell Heroes*.

Crowther Street

This steep cobbled street lies off Middle Hillgate. In 1930 painter L. S. Lowry captured its appearance in a painting now kept in Stockport's Art Gallery. Traditionally, it had been referred to as 'Bombers Brow' on account of the fact that its residents were in the habit of doing 'moonlight flits', i.e. rapid removals in advance of the expected bailiffs when families were in serious debt.

Lowry worked for the Pall Mall Property Company in Manchester as a rent collector and his work would have taken him to many streets like this. Nowadays, it is a much more respectable place, the houses being renovated in 2004. The street featured several times in the recent film about Lowry and his mother.

Crowther Street, off Middle Hillgate.

D

Daly, Tess

The model, novelist and television presenter was born in Stockport in 1969 but was brought up in New Mills in Derbyshire.

Having been 'scouted' whilst waiting outside a McDonald's restaurant, she had her first professional assignment aged just eighteen in Tokyo. A number of assignments across Asia and Europe followed and she spent times based in Paris, London and New York.

Her television career started after a New York friend suggested she tried interviewing a few 'red carpet' celebrities. After contacting the producers of Channel 4's *The Big Breakfast* with a sample recording, she was asked to co-host the 'Find Me a Model' competition. Other shows followed including *Home of Their Own* and, from 2004, BBC 1's *Strictly Come Dancing*, latterly with Claudia Winkleman.

She has also written novels, the first being *The Camera Never Lies*, which was published in 2011.

Tess Daly arriving at the *Strictly Come Dancing* launch at Television Centre, London, 11 September 2012. (Simon Burchill/Shutterstock)

Davenport Park

Occasionally referred to as Stockport's 'Secret Suburb', this is a small area to the west of Buxton Road, comprising a mere three roads, two of which are named Davenport Park Road and the third Clifton Park Road. There is a single vehicular access from Buxton Road.

The park was and is a gated residential community, although the main gate is not staffed and free though conditional vehicular access is allowed.

The area is named after the Davenports of Bramall Hall (see separate entry) and it was part of the 1877 disposal of the estate for development purposes. The purchaser in this case was a John Simpson of Stockport, who bought it for £8,500.

In 1858 the Stockport, Disley and Whaley Bridge Railway Company built Davenport Station. This followed a complaint from Colonel William Davenport that the railway company had not honoured a promise to provide a station at Bramhall Lane. The station was not initially successful, and closed the following year; however, it reopened in 1862. In due course the station helped increase the attractiveness of the park for residential development.

Clifton Park Road in Davenport Park.

The three roads were developed between the 1890s and the end of the 1930s. The early houses included substantial villas, many of which remain today. Initial building was on the outer sides of the triangle formed by the three roads. Trees line all the roads, and the overall density of development is low, helping maintain the special character of the place.

The roads and common parts of the park were not publicly adopted and were meant to be made up and maintained by the residents themselves. This did not happen at first, and the roads gradually became quagmires. After 1901, when the area was absorbed into the Borough of Stockport, things began to change. In 1906, the local authority threatened to make them up at the cost of the residents and adopt them. In August that year a Davenport Park Roads Committee was formed by the residents with each householder paying their share of the cost together with an annual levy for their maintenance. The roads had all been surfaced by the following year. This way of proceeding allowed the roads to remain private roads and gave residents control over access.

That remains the case today, with the committee renamed the Davenport Park Committee. Some of the earlier villas were demolished several decades ago and flats built on their sites. The Junior department of Stockport Grammar School also occupies some the road frontage but the essential character of the park remains. It is now a Conservation Area.

Signs at the entrance to Davenport Park from the A6.

Dickinson, David

The television presenter and antiques expert was born on Cheadle Heath in August 1941. He was born out of wedlock to an Armenian woman, Eugenie Gulesserian. At an early age, he was placed for adoption and settled with a local family, the Dickinsons.

Initially working as an apprentice at a local aircraft factory, by the age of eighteen David was working in the cloth trade in Manchester. For some time, he ran a shop of his own. After closing this in 1991, he spent his time selling antiques at fairs, including locations such as Olympia.

His television career took off in 1998 when the BBC made a two-part programme about him and his work preparing for a fair at Olympia. He went on to star as an expert on antiques on shows such as *This Morning* and *The Antiques Show*, and then presenting *Bargain Hunt.* In 2006, he moved over to ITV where *Dickinson's Real Deal* was broadcast. He has also made a number of guest appearances on shows such as *I'm a Celebrity, Get Me Out of Here* and *Ant and Dec's Saturday Night Takeaway.* He also traced his own ancestry on the programme *Who Do You Think You Are.*

Two of his trademarks are his tanned appearance – quite genuine by the way, and originating from his part-Armenian parentage – and various catchphrases he uses, such as 'a real bobby-dazzler' and 'cheap as chips', the latter to signify a real bargain.

David Dickinson (on the left) arriving at the ITV Palooza event at the Royal Festival Hall, 16 October 2018. (Featureflash photo agency/Shutterstock)

E

St Elisabeth's Church, Reddish

This church was built between 1881 and 1883 as part of Sir William Houldsworth's plan for Reddish village (see separate entry) and paid for entirely by him. The architect was Alfred Waterhouse, designer of Manchester Town Hall and other notable buildings.

The church is named after Houldsworth's wife. It is also spelt with an 's' rather than the more usual 'z' as there is no Saint Elizabeth. In line with Sir William's own preferences, the church is an Anglo-Catholic church.

The church is grand in scale and is made of Openshaw brick with Wrexham stone dressings. A set of Stations of the Cross, which include depictions of Stockport Viaduct and Pendlebury Hall formerly on nearby Lancashire Hill, were commissioned from Graeme Wilson in 1983.

The church has a large organ by William Hill & Co. of London, originally with three manuals. It was reduced in size to two manuals in the 1960s, but surprisingly, much of the pipework of the discarded manual was retained within the organ loft. Some of this was reused in the most recent restoration of the instrument.

An adjoining rectory was built in 1874. This has now been replaced by a more modern building and the original building is now used as nursery accommodation for the adjoining primary school.

St Elisabeth's Church, Reddish. View from junction of Leamington Road and St Elisabeth's Way.

Etherow Country Park and Compstall Village

Compstall Mill and its adjacent village were developed by the Andrew family after 1820, and in some respects Compstall was a model industrial village run by a benevolent owner. For the village's inhabitants, they built an Athenaeum (for many years used as a library and museum), shops, St Peter's Church, a Wesleyan Methodist Chapel, and in 1825 for themselves, Compstall Hall, on the road to nearby Romiley.

A large mill reservoir or 'lodge' was dug to serve the mill's waterwheels, and was supplied with water from the River Goyt via a navigable canal or mill leat that led from the still-impressive weir around a mile up the valley.

This leat, not connected to the rest of the canal system, was used to transport coal mined from small pits up the valley, at a time when steam power was used to supplement the original water power. The tub boats, of which these remains are an example, were made of riveted cast-iron plates. Approximately 22 feet long, 16 feet 5 inches wide and 3 feet deep, they could carry around 8 tons of coal. They would have been drawn by horse, which would have pulled several barges for each trip. One lies derelict in the mud near to the weir.

The mill ceased to be used for textile purposes in 1966, but the use of the navigation has ended much earlier, possibly at the time when the mill was fully converted to electricity in 1915. It is said that the boat was first placed here in the 1920s.

In the 1970s, proposals were made to rescue this barge and renovate it, but it still remains here, quietly rusting away.

The remains of the inclined tramways used for transporting the coal to the leat and the abutments of the former bridge which carried the tramway over the Goyt can still be traced.

The country park is one of the oldest in England.

Main lake at Etherow Country Park.

The rusting remains of an old coal barge at Etherow Country Park.

Housing at Compstall village on Montague Street.

The weir in Etherow Country Park.

Farm Produce Hall

This is another of Stockport's market buildings, and actually pre-dates the Market Hall opposite, being opened in 1852 on the site of the town's first Post Office. The building cost £4,200 and is in a neoclassical style.

At various times, the building has been known as the Produce Hall, the Cheese Market and the Hen Market. Stockport's first public library opened in the upper floor of the building in 1875.

Both Edward VII and George V were pronounced as Kings of the country from the building's balcony.

The building has recently been converted into a food and drinks venue.

Farm Produce Hall in the Market Place.

Fielding, Yvette

The television presenter, producer and actress was born in Manchester but was raised in Bramhall, attending Bramhall High School, Hillcrest Grammar School and Stockport Convent school, among others. She was born in Manchester in 1968.

In June 1987, she became a presenter on BBC's *Blue Peter*; at the age of eighteen she became the youngest ever presenter on the show, a role which continued for five years. During her early television years, she made many appearances and in 2004 was named Multi-Channel Personality of the Year by the Variety Club.

From 2002, Fielding and her husband founded their own production company, Antix Productions, which specialised in investigating the paranormal. Shows such as *Most Haunted* and *Ghosthunting with ...* followed. She became a cult figure and established herself as British television's 'first lady of the paranormal'. She has also written *Archie the Ghost Hunter*.

For a few years until 2016 she ran and co-owned a tea shop near Manchester Cathedral called Propertea.

Foster, Norman

The renowned architect was born in 1935 in Reddish. At an early date the family moved to Manchester. Attending a local grammar school, his first job was in the Treasurer's department of the local authority, before joining the Royal Air Force as part of his national service.

His introduction to architecture was as a contract manager with a local architect's firm and from 1955 to 1961 he studied architecture at Manchester University, which was followed by time at the Yale School of Architecture where he earned a master's degree and met his future business partner, Richard Rogers.

Sir Norman Foster at the opening of the Philological Library faculties at the Free University of Berlin-Dahlem, 14 September 2005. (360b/Shutterstock)

In 1963, Foster, Rogers and others formed Team 4 as an architectural practice. This dissolved in 1967, after which Foster Associates was born.

From the mid-1970s onwards, the practice began producing designs for notable buildings, including the Willis Building in Ipswich, The Sainsbury's Centre for the Visual Arts in Norwich, the terminal building at Stansted Airport (1990) and a number of buildings abroad.

More recent work has included the London 'Gherkin', the Millau Bridge in France, the reconstruction of the Berlin Reichstag, and work on Apple Park in the USA.

He has received a number of awards and in July 1999 he was created Baron Foster of Thomas Bank in Reddish. The author is unaware of any buildings in Stockport that he or his practice may have designed.

Foy, Claire

The actress was born in Stockport in 1984, but was brought up in Manchester, Leeds and Buckinghamshire. After attending grammar school in Aylesbury, she went on to study drama and screen studies at Liverpool John Moores University and the Oxford School of Drama.

After 2008, she began to appear on the stage and screen, playing roles such as Amy Dorrit in *Little Dorrit*, Lady Persephone in the revival of *Upstairs Downstairs* and as Anne Boleyn in the serial *Wolf Hall*.

Even greater public and international recognition came in 2016 when she played the young Queen Elizabeth II in the first two series of the Netflix drama *The Crown*. For this role, she won a number of awards, including the Golden Globe Award for Best Actress – Television Series Drama.

Claire Foy attending the photocall for the film *First Man* at the 75th Venice Biennale, 29 August 2018. (Dennis Makarenko/Shutterstock)

Goyt Hall

This is one of Stockport's lesser-known buildings. It is located in the Goyt Valley, near to Otterspool Bridge, and was built by Randal Davenport around 1570. It has a Tudor appearance, being half-timbered.

In 1664, the hall came into the ownership of Sir Fulke Lucy, related to Sir Thomas Lucy, who was associated with William Shakespeare's younger days. When Manchester City Council were building their nearby Bredbury overspill estate in the 1960s, it was nicknamed the 'Shakespeare Estate' after the names given to many of its streets.

It was substantially altered around 1860 by R. Horsefield and is now a farmhouse. A proposed road link, on the plans for many years, linking the A6 at High Lane with the M60 at Bredbury would substantially affect this property.

It remains a private property and close access is not advisable without prior permission.

Goyt Hall, Bredbury.

The Guernsey Connection

Shortly before the German occupation of the Channel Islands on 30 June 1940, thousands of Channel Islanders were evacuated to mainland Britain, particularly from Guernsey and Alderney. Mostly, these were women and children, together with young men suitable for service with the Forces or in munition production.

Stockport saw the greatest number of such evacuees in one town. Around 1,200 came to the old County Borough area and when the area of the present metropolitan borough and adjoining High Peak areas are included the total rises to over 2,000. All would have come by train from Weymouth.

The wide streets, traffic, and railway viaduct were overwhelming to people, most of whom had never left their island before, and where life was carried out on a much smaller scale. However, in due course, they all integrated into normal society and many of the survivors have happy memories of their time in the town. Some even stayed at the end of the war.

In 2015, a special service was held in St Mary's Parish Church to commemorate the seventieth anniversary of the island's liberation. A few of the former evacuees came over and helped in the singing of 'Sarnia Cherie', the Guernsey national anthem.

This plaque, on the wall outside the station, commemorates the part the town played in accommodating them.

Memorial plaque to the Guernsey evacuees, Stockport Station.

H

Halliday Hill House

This Grade II listed building, in reality quite a small cottage, dates from medieval times. Its claim to fame is that for several hundred years, up to the middle of the nineteenth century, it was the ancestral home of the Dodge family. The family were very influential at various times and some seventeen members of the family were mayors of Stockport over the years.

Two Dodge brothers emigrated to Salem, Massachusetts, in 1629 and the family name spread far and wide in the New World in the years that followed, although others with the same name also emigrated from other parts of England. Various places in the USA as well as the Dodge Motors brand are named after the family. Today a Friendship Charter exists between Stockport and Dodge City.

Close access is not possible.

Halliday Hill House, Offerton.

Harrytown Hall, Bredbury.

Harrytown Hall

Still known to many as Harrytown Convent, this building is a former manor house. The original building, dating from the fifteenth century, was built by Harry Buckshaw. In 1671 it was replaced by the present building and it remains remarkably well preserved. The initials of John and Sarah Buckshaw, who had arranged for the rebuilding, are carved over the front entrance doorway, along with the date.

The hall was later owned by the Foster and Walton families and in 1913 it became a convent school. This use continued until 1978 when the school moved out, becoming Harrytown Catholic High School in the process on the adjoining site.

The hall itself has since been divided into flats.

The Hatters

Stockport County Football Club was first formed in 1883 as Heaton Norris Rovers by members of the Heaton Norris Congregational Church. They played at a ground on Green Lane, Heaton Norris, and were nicknamed 'The Hatters' from the outset due to the town's importance in the hat-making industry. The current name was adopted in 1890.

The club became part of the Football League in 1900, playing in the second division. In 1902, they moved to their present site at Edgeley Park.

The club has played in the lower divisions for many years of its history, with occasional periods in higher places. The current main stand was built in 1936. In the mid -1970s, for a brief period they had George Best on the team; it marked his last appearances as a professional player.

Edgeley Park,
home of
'The Hatters'.

The 1990s were a period of success for the club and at one point they reached the semi-final of the League Cup. There have been several changes of ownership and the club seems to alternate between periods in the sporting doldrums and spells of moderate success.

The ground has also played a part in the development of Rugby League. In a match that took place on 7 September 1895 against Brighouse, Stockport played their first home game under the rules of Rugby League (then known as the Northern Union).

Hatton, Ricky

Ricky Hatton was born in Stockport in 1978, but grew up on the Hattersley overspill estate in neighbouring Hyde. Whilst still young, he had a trial with the youth team of Rochdale football club, where both his father and grandfather had played.

He joined a boxing club in Hyde to train and at the age of fourteen he saw a fight at Old Trafford between Nigel Benn and Chris Eubank. On leaving school, he was taken on in the family carpet business, but after he cut four fingers with a Stanley knife, his father made him a salesman for the firm.

Between 1994 and 1997, Hatton boxed as an amateur. He trained at the Moss Side, Manchester, gym of Billy 'The Preacher' Graham. In 1996, he represented the UK in the AIBA Youth World Boxing Championship, but was eliminated in the semi-finals. Controversy surrounded this decision, and when it was later found that one of the judges had accepted a bribe, Hatton became disillusioned with the amateur game and decided to become professional, which he did at the age of eighteen, fighting Colin McAuley at Widnes, a game which he won. His second fight was at New York's Madison Square Garden. Hatton was named Young Boxer of the Year in 1999 by the British Boxing Writers' Club.

From 2006 he alternated between the Welterweight and Light Welterweight categories several times. In 2007, he was defeated for the first time in his career by Floyd Mayweather and two years later by Manny Pacquiao. He retired from the sport in 2011, but announced a comeback the following year. Following a defeat by Vyacheslav Senchenko, he retired for a second and final time. His overall record in the sport was forty-three wins and three defeats.

Outside the ring, Hatton has made a name for himself. He is a lifelong supporter of Manchester City Football Club and his entrance music was the club's song 'Blue Moon', sung by the band Supra. Between fights, Hatton allowed himself to put on weight and is sometimes referred to by his fans as 'Ricky Fatton', a name he parodied himself.

He has made several television appearances, and hosted a chat show, *Ricky Speaks*, for a time. He was awarded the MBE for services to sports in 2007. He also runs Hatton Promotions, which promotes the game, and he is involved with training and charitable activities.

Hat Works

Stockport was once the centre of the British hatting industry and this museum, spread over two floors, gives a good overview of the industry. It opened in 2000, having spent a few years operating in part of the former Battersby hat works in Offerton.

It is located in Wellington Mill, adjoining the A6, which was built in 1830–31 as a fireproof cotton-spinning mill. The building was taken over by Ward Bros in 1895 and it began to be used for hat manufacture, which continued until the 1930s.

Hat Museum, main entrance on Wellington Road South.

During the Middle Ages, Stockport had gradually developed as a centre for the silk industry and hat making. The eighteenth century saw the mechanisation of the silk industry and the same happened to hat making in the nineteenth century, making Stockport the leading national centre for the industry, closely followed by nearby Denton.

The industry began to decline after 1918, although more than 3,000 were still being employed in 1932, the third largest employer in the town after textiles and engineering. Thereafter changing social habits and fashion placed the industry in a state of continuous decline. In 1966, the remaining four largest hat makers amalgamated to form Associated British Hat Manufacturers. The final factory in Stockport was closed in 1997.

Hiller, Wendy

English actress Wendy Hiller was born in Bramhall in August 1912. Her parents were relatively well-off and sent her to Winceby House School in Bexhill, Sussex, where she mastered speech and refinement. At the age of eighteen she became an apprentice at the Manchester Repertory Theatre. Initially working as an assistant stage manager, at first she took on minor roles with her professional debut being in *The Ware Case* in 1930.

Her acting breakthrough came in 1934 when she played the role of Sally Hardcastle in *Love on the Dole*. The play was taken on tour and it was during one of the London performances the following year that she caught the attention of the playwright George Bernard Shaw. As a result, she starred in his plays *Saint Joan* and *Pygmalion* in 1936 at the Malvern Festival. The year 1938 saw her first film appearance in the film version of *Pygmalion*; she received an Oscar nomination for her portrayal of Eliza Doolittle.

Her career expanded in the following decades with several film, television and stage roles, including Broadway appearances. Appearing in the film *Separate Tables* in 1959 won her an Academy Award for Best Supporting Actress. However, she made the stage her main priority throughout her career. In her later years, she played many grande dame roles.

She was awarded the OBE in 1971 and became a Dame four years later. Her final stage role, in 1988, was in *Driving Miss Daisy*, when she played an elderly American Jewish southerner and her final film role was in *The Countess Alice* in 1993. She died in 2003.

The Hillgates and Little Underbank

Namely, Little Underbank (closest to the town centre), Lower Hillgate, Middle Hillgate and Higher Hillgate, these were Stockport's 'main road' to the south before the construction of the Wellington Road 'by-pass' in 1819–20. Little Underbank and Lower Hillgate are the narrowest but contain the most interesting buildings, the buildings become progressively more mundane as you travel south.

Little Underbank contains Winter's Clockhouse (see separate entry) and is crossed by the striking St Petersgate Bridge which connects St Petersgate to Market Place, and which is also connected to the street below by way of pedestrian steps. This cast-iron bridge opened in February 1868 and was designed by R. Rawlinson. It is also known as the Angel Bridge and cost £10,500. The span of the bridge is 27 feet 3 inches long and the bridge bears the borough's coat of arms.

A couple of other interesting streets also connect Lower Hillgate to the market area. Where Little Underbank joins Lower Hillgate is Mealhouse Brow, at one time known as Wynn Hill or Wynn Bank, which was one of the historic access routes into the market and Stockport's castle. The medieval Old Dungeon, closed in 1790, is at the top, being located underneath the old Court Leet building, which served as both a court and as a town hall, before becoming a grain store, after which the street is now named. The entrance to the Dungeon is still visible at the side of the sweeping steps at the top of the Brow, and is now open to the public one day a month courtesy of the Stockport Heritage Trust. The building on top of it contains what is now Stockport's only nineteenth-century double-fronted shop window.

The town's bakehouse was located at the lower end of the street.

The other street connecting to the market is Rostron Brow, formerly called Rosen Bank, after farmer Ralph Rosen who was born at the lower end. This was formerly a street of ill repute, with many alehouses. One called 'The Dust Hole', formerly the Schofield Inn, was the most popular, and closed in 1896.

Robinsons Brewery is also located on Lower Hillgate (see separate entry). St Thomas's Church (see separate entry) is located off Higher Hillgate.

Little Underbank, with the St Petersgate Bridge in the background.

Above: Mealhouse Brow, top end, showing the 'Dungeon'.

Right: Rostron Brow.

I

Former Stockport Infirmary

This used to be a main hospital for the Stockport area before gradually being supplanted by Stepping Hill Hospital further south along the A6.

First opened in 1792 as a dispensary, it was rebuilt as an infirmary, opening in July 1833 by the architect Richard Lane. Subsequent extensions were built in 1871, 1900, 1914 and 1938. It was built on land donated by Lady Vernon, is built in a Greek Doric style and is a Grade II listed building. Its use as a hospital is reputedly why bells were never installed in the bell tower of the Town Hall just over the road.

It ceased to be used as a hospital in 1996 and is currently used as offices, called Millennium House.

The former Stockport Infirmary on Wellington Road South.

Jennison Family Tomb, Cheadle

In the churchyard to the rear of St Mary's Church stands this imposing tomb to the Jennison family, who created Belle Vue, the large zoo and amusement park in east Manchester which closed down in stages between 1977 and 1981. Originating from Nottingham, the family moved to Macclesfield and by 1815 were living at Adswood where Jennison's Strawberry Gardens were created in the 1820s (see entry for Monkey Bridge).

From 1836, the family lived mainly at the Hyde Road site in Manchester, although some of the family continued to live at Adswood until the 1840s.

Belle Vue went from strength to strength and in due course, parts of the extended family moved to more affluent areas, including parts of present-day Stockport.

This tomb contains many members of the family, including John himself, his wife Maria and many of their children and their spouses. One who is not included is his eldest son, John, who was excluded from the succession to Belle Vue and who is buried in a tomb in Wilmslow churchyard.

Jennison family tomb, Cheadle Churchyard.

K

Keegan, Michelle

Michelle Keegan was born in Stockport although she attended secondary school in Eccles. Later she attended the Manchester School of Acting.

After spells of working at the Trafford Centre and as a check-in agent at Manchester Airport, on her second audition she was offered the role of Tina McIntyre in *Coronation Street* in 2007 and she remained with the show until 2014, taking part in some 861 episodes. In 2010, she was listed by the *Guardian* as one of the ten best *Coronation Street* characters of all time.

More recently, she has starred as plucky army medic Corporal Georgie Lane in the BBC TV drama series *Our Girl*. She has taken part in many other television, film and radio shows.

Michelle Keegan arriving at the 2011 Soap Awards at the former Granada TV studios in Manchester. (Simon Burchell/Featureflash photo agency/ Shutterstock)

L

Lancashire Bridge

This bridge stands at one end of the Merseyway shopping precinct and marks the historic boundary between Lancashire and Cheshire. It is also close to the place where the rivers Goyt and Etherow join to become the River Mersey.

The present bridge dates from 1891 and replaced others dating back to 1282. In 2015 it was restored and opened out so that more of it can be seen.

Lancashire Bridge in the town centre at the eastern end of the Merseyway shopping centre.

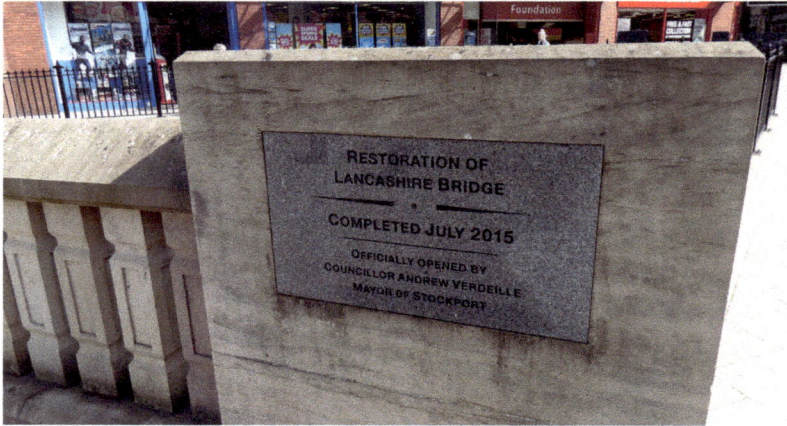

Plaque marking the restoration of Lancashire Bridge.

Lime kilns, Marple

Associated with the Peak Forest Canal are the Marple Lime Kilns. These formerly occupied a large area bounded by the canal and the Marple-New Mills road, and had their own canal branch from Posset Bridge. They were finished in 1797 and were another product of Samuel Oldknow.

It is said that Oldknow built the lime kilns to provide work for the husbands of the women he employed at Mellor Mill. Although the lime kilns were not profitable for Oldknow they continued in use until the early years of the twentieth century, and were even lived in at various times.

The Lime Kilns, Marple.

The front wall of the kilns occupied a very visible site, and was therefore provided with windows with Gothic-style tracery to improve the façade's appearance, although this was offset by the kilns' six chimneys. The kilns comprised four large tunnels running into the canal bank. The limestone was fed into the top of the kilns at canal level and the burnt lime was then removed into dispatching buildings, which survive nearby as housing.

The pleasantly landscaped remains we see today are only a limited reminder of the area's industrial past. They give little indication of the former Gothic façade of the kilns themselves as work done in the mid-1970s involved bricking-up some of the tunnels and hiding some of the masonry.

Lyme Park and Hall

Of course, Lyme Park is not within the boundaries of Stockport Metropolitan Borough so some should argue that it should not be within this book. The counter arguments to that are that it is relatively close to the present-day borough and that it was Stockport Corporation's agreement in 1946 to become involved in the running of the park that was crucial in helping save the park and hall for the nation under the care of the National Trust.

The land that forms the park had been granted, along with much other land, by the Crown to the Legh family in 1398, when the old Macclesfield Royal Hunting Forest was dispersed. That grant was in place of a perpetual pension of forty marks granted to Sir Thomas Danyers in recognition of his bravery and patriotism shown at the Battle of Crecy in 1346, when he recovered the English Standard (a small flag) which had fallen into French hands.

By the mid-1400s, the present park had been enclosed and a hunting lodge built at its centre. That lodge was itself replaced by the first part of the present-day hall, built in the late Elizabethan period, some features of which survive today. Extensions followed in the mid-1600s and considerable alterations undertaken around 1715 by the Italian architect Giacomo Leoni. Many of the hall's façades, particularly those fronting the Reflecting Lake and the interior of the courtyard, reflect this work. Further extensions were carried out under Thomas Legh using the architect Thomas Wyatt in the early 1800s.

The hall's interiors are sumptuous, with a Long Gallery, a 1700s Saloon with elaborate carvings reputedly by Grinling Gibbons (though today doubted) and a very attractive Library which contains the unique Lyme Missal, the only near-complete surviving copy of a pre-Reformation missal and the most valuable book ever purchased by the National Trust. The parkland is quite varied, ranging from formal gardens to windswept moorland. Many have become familiar with the hall's surroundings by virtue of the fact that the hall formed the exterior of 'Pemberley' in the BBC's 1994 adaptation of *Pride and Prejudice*, and the more recent spoof advert for Warburtons bread starring comedian Peter Kay.

Lyme Hall, main elevation viewed over the Reflecting Lake.

The hall is not surrounded by a large collection of 'follies' but a couple of buildings are worth a mention.

Set prominently on a ridge overlooking the main entrance driveway, Lyme Cage is said to have its origins from around 1524. One theory holds that it was built even earlier, during the Wars of the Roses, as a watchtower. One of its early uses was to apprehend poachers before being taken for trial, which is probably why it has acquired its name.

In 1733–37, it was reconstructed to a design by Leoni, engaged in reconstruction work on the hall at the time. It is said that the Cage was also used as a vantage point for hunting or military purposes (the Home Guard used it during the Second World War).

It was latterly occupied by estate keepers (who lived in the upper floors) until around 1920 and it was bricked up circa 1947.

Three of the elevations contain sundials (giving the time by Greenwich Mean Time) with inscriptions in Latin or English. It is rumoured that an underground passage links the Cage with the hall, but there is no evidence in support of this. The Cage is some 848 feet above sea level.

Some restoration work was carried out in the late 1980s, followed by a more complete scheme ten years later. The interior is now open on some Sunday afternoons.

 Located on rising ground towards the eastern edges of the park is another curious structure known as the Lantern. Sometimes called the Lanthorn Tower, this structure is less well known than the Cage. Its name derives from its shape: three storeys in height with a triangular roof, with an archway on the lowest floor.

Above left: The 'Cage', Lyme Park.

Above right: Lanthorn Tower, Lyme Park.

It was originally located on the roof of the Elizabethan hall, but was taken down and re-erected here, as a focal point, when Leoni was undertaking his alterations in the eighteenth century. In recent years, some restoration of the stonework has taken place and visitors can now access the interior.

The fortunes of the Legh family reached a high point during the Edwardian period and declined sharply after the First World War, when their coal royalty income from the Lancashire coalfield began to decline. Despite measures taken in 1920 to minimize death duties, by the time of the Second World War, they could no longer afford the upkeep of the estate and they were seeking to pass the property to the National Trust. This finally occurred when Stockport Corporation agreed to take a ninety-nine-year lease of the property. Stockport took over the day-to-day running of the property and ran it until 1994, when management was taken back 'in-house' by the Trust.

The park and hall make for an enjoyable day out and are well worth visiting, though do check opening times and days. Visitors to the hall can avail themselves of free Regency costume hire for the day and play out their own 'Elizabeth and Darcy' fantasies in the house and gardens.

Market

A market has operated in Stockport since 1260, when a charter was granted by Prince Edward, Earl of Chester, to Robert de Stokeport III, Lord of the Manor. Initially, the charter allowed a market to take place very Thursday, together with a yearly fair lasting eight days beginning on St Wilfred's Day, the 12th October.

The weekly market had been moved to Fridays by the seventeenth century. It sold farm produce and was also held on Saturdays by 1810. Early markets used open-air stalls, with perhaps some use of adjacent buildings as well. As time passed, more specialised buildings were erected, with a 'Market House', a colonnaded building with four gables, existing by 1680 before being removed sometime after 1770. A New Market House was commissioned by Lord Vernon in 1842, but had a short life, being demolished around 1851.

The present-day Market Hall in the centre of Market Place originates from 1860 when the Manorial Tolls Committee opted to accept a design from James Heywood of Derby, from among nine submitted. The design was for a covered space formed by iron columns and a glass roof, without sides, and cost £2,770. It was referred to as 'The Glass Umbrella' and opened in 1862.

Stockport Market, main building.

In 1896, one of the stallholders, Ephraim Marks, sought permission to enclose his stall, and others soon followed. The entire perimeter had been enclosed by 1910. By 1908, Ephraim Marks had become one of the shareholders in Marks and Spencer Ltd. The westernmost bay of the building was removed in 1912.

A programme of repairs and restoration was undertaken by the council in 1985, and further work and substantial improvements were carried out in 2008.

McInnerny, Tim

The television, film and theatre actor was born in Cheadle Hulme in 1956, but was brought up in Stroud. He went to Wadham College, Oxford.

He is best known for his comic appearances, one of his first being in 1983 as Lord Percy Percy in the series *Blackadder*. Later, in the same series he appeared as Captain Darling. Other roles have included Lord Robert Gower in the HBO series *Game of Thrones*. His most recent television appearance was as a Chief Whip in the 2020 production *The Trial of Christine Keeler*.

Merseyway

To many people today, the name Merseyway equates to the shopping centre of the same name, built in 1965 by the developers Hammerson.

General view of the Merseyway shopping centre from the west.

However, it was also the name of a new road, built on the same site in 1939 on stilts over the River Mersey, and which replaced Princes Street and Chestergate as the town's main east-west thoroughfares.

The centre replaced the road and has undergone a number of refurbishments since 1965. At the end of the 1990s, the covered part at the western end was extended, although most of the centre remains uncovered, which puts it at a disadvantage compared to newer shopping centres. It attracts some 14 million visitors a year.

Hammerson sold the centre in 2003 and from 2009 it was placed in receivership.

Alongside, from 2017, is the new Redrock development comprising 'The Light' cinema, a gymnasium and some eateries. This won the 2018 Carbuncle Cup for Britain's ugliest new building.

Monkey Bridge, Adswood

Many older readers will remember Belle Vue Zoo and Amusement Park, located on Hyde Road, Manchester, which operated from 1836 until its gradual closure between 1977 and 1982. Belle Vue had its origins in Adswood, on a site next to this bridge now covered by a modern residential development.

Belle Vue was founded by John Jennison and in 1815 his father built a house on the half-acre plot here. John himself took over ten years later and soon after opened the gardens on Sunday afternoons, calling them the 'Strawberry Gardens' or 'Jennison's Gardens'. By 1828/29, the enterprise had become a full-time occupation and a small animal collection, mainly birds, had been added, together with a brewhouse. The original house became a pub, the 'Adam and Eve'. By the mid-1830s, the success of the enterprise encouraged Jennison to think bigger, and realising that he could expand no more on the restricted Adswood site, he took a lease of the Hyde Road site in 1836, finally closing Adswood the following year.

He did however retain ownership and in the early 1840s, installed his eldest son as manager and reopened the gardens, this time with monkeys included among the

Monkey Bridge, Adswood, with the original site of Jennison's Strawberry Gardens in the left background.

animal collection. This exercise was short-lived. However, it is from this later time, and not earlier, that the site acquired its local nickname 'The Monkey House' and the adjoining railway bridge 'The Monkey Bridge'.

Mount Tabor Chapel Column Capitals

The four detailed stone capitals in this small paved garden and rest area opposite the Town Hall are all that remains of the former Mount Tabor Methodist Chapel, a substantial building that stood on this site.

The chapel was built when members of the earlier Mount Tabor Chapel in Middle Hillgate, part of the Methodist 'New Connexion' branch, outgrew their premises. Constructed between October 1865 and May 1869 at a cost of over £9,000, the new building could seat 900 worshippers. The main entrance at the front was up a massive flight of steps that extended across the front of the building. This supported a lofty portico consisting of four columns topped by these Corinthian capitals, hewn from Darley Dale stone.

Underneath the building were rooms used by the chapel's Sunday school, which at its height had thirty-eight teachers for its 278 boys and girls. During the Second World War, the Sunday school rooms were used as the local food rationing office, and later as temporary offices of the local authority's housing department.

The chapel was demolished in 1969 but had not been used for religious purposes for some time, since the remaining congregation had joined the Trinity Methodist Church. The column capitals have been moved around at least twice in recent decades and have now been joined by the statue commemorating James Conway, one of the 'Cockleshell Heroes'.

Columns capitals from the former Mount Tabor Chapel, at the junction of Wellington Road South and Edward Street.

N

Alan Newton Way

Alan Newton was born in Adswood, Stockport, in 1931. In 1946 he joined the Stockport Road Club and from 1952 he competed in international events for running, winning a Bronze medal for the 4,000 metres team pursuit event at the Helsinki Olympics held that year. He became the first Stockport citizen to win an Olympic medal.

His achievements went largely unnoticed until 2012 when the London Olympics held that year led to a search for previous Olympic medallists from Stockport. He was invited to open a new bridge across the River Goyt provided by Stockport Council and Sustrans. He also received several invitations to events, including one for 300 past Olympians held at the Mansion House in London. In 2016 a new cycle route along the Goyt Valley, named the Alan Newton Way, opened between Marple Hall Drive and Bredbury. It was originally intended to reach Marple Bridge.

This photo shows the start of the trail on Marple Dale Road. In the background is a headstone from Marple Hall, which stood nearby until demolished in 1959.

Above left: Finger posts for Alan Newton Way, Marple.

Above right: Memorial stone to the former Marple Hall.

O

Ockleston Memorial, Cheadle

This memorial, originally a drinking fountain, dates from 1889 and commemorates Robert Ockleston, a well-liked doctor in the village who had died the previous year. The memorial was unveiled by the Lord of the Manor, James Watts, in April 1889, when it was formally handed over to the local Board.

Originally located in front of the George and Dragon, it was moved in 1967 to allow for road widening and relocated to the entrance to Queen's Gardens. More recently, it has been repositioned again, rather closer to its original location.

The memorial originally comprised several elements. There was a water trough for horses and a Gothic-style street lamp. There were also four smaller troughs, designed for smaller animals such as dogs. The water fountains themselves were covered by gabled stone canopies.

Ockleston Memorial, Cheadle.

Oldknow, Samuel

Samuel Oldknow was born in Anderton, Lancashire, and it was there in the early 1780s that he commenced as a muslin manufacturer. In the following years, his enterprises grew rapidly and he acquired factories in Stockport and the surrounding areas. In 1787 he purchased the Bottoms Hall Estate between Marple and Mellor, and on it he built Mellor Mill, arguably his crowning achievement.

Oldknow was also involved in the Peak Forest Canal as its principal promoter, improvements to local roads, coal mining and the building of the Marple Lime Kilns. After 1793, his businesses were beset by financial problems and many were sold off or leased out. Oldknow died in 1828 but his mill remained in production until 1892, when it was destroyed by fire.

This circular headstone is located in the Memorial Park in the centre of Marple. It is close to the old Marple stocks and an old sundial which came from the long-demolished Marple Hall. The headstone, from Mellor Mill, bears Oldknow's initials and the date 1790, when construction work on the mill started.

Excavated remains of Oldknow's Mellor Mill.

On the Mellor Mill site itself, accessible on the way to the Roman Lakes, considerable excavations have been carried out since 2009 under the auspices of the Mellor Archaeological Trust to uncover what remains of the mill and these can be viewed by the public.

The walls at the north end of the mill have been uncovered and debris has been cleared from the Wellington wheelpit at the centre of the mill. Other clearance has included the cobbled area in front of the mill and the 100-metre tunnel which held the drive shaft from the Waterloo wheel. In early 2019 a replica date stone to the same design as the original in the Marple Memorial Gardens was installed at the site.

The archaeological work is ongoing. The Trust organises specialist guided tours of the site and the surrounding Bottoms Hall Estate.

Replica headstone from Mellor Mill.

The original Mellor Mill headstone in Marple Memorial Park.

Peak Forest Canal

The canal locks and junction between the Peak Forest and Macclesfield canals at Marple are a popular destination for Sunday afternoon walks. At the canal junction is this graceful 'roving bridge', built for the days when canal narrowboats were pulled by horses.

The bridge is designed to allow a northbound horse pulling a boat from the Macclesfield Canal to cross the canal from then towpath on the eastern side of the canal onto the Peak Forest Canal (which was on the western side) without the boatmen having to unhitch the towing line from the horse as it crossed the bridge. The same advantage of course applied in the reverse direction.

Stop lock at the junction of the Macclesfield and Peak Forest Canals, Marple.

The old 'stop lock' on the Macclesfield Canal, now no longer used, was designed to prevent one canal company getting 'free' water from its neighbour. An old toll office stands on the bridge itself, and has recently been converted into a mini visitor centre.

Further down the canal locks stands Posset Bridge, where the main road crosses the canal. The curiously named bridge was built by Samuel Oldknow in 1794. The name is said to have been based on the fact that he allowed his workforce a 'posset' of ale from his public house, the Navigation Inn, which formerly adjoined the canal.

The bridge itself has two small tunnels, one to gain access by foot to the adjoining lock gates, and the other (shown here) to take the canal towpath under the roadway.

A short way down the canal, near the road that leads from Marple to Marple Bridge, is an attractive warehouse, now put to other uses, complete with boat-loading hole that Oldknow built to serve Mellor Mill.

The locks change the level of the Peak Forest Canal by some 214 feet. The flight was opened for use in 1804, although the canal had been finished a few years earlier, with a temporary tramroad linking the upper and lower section until the locks were completed.

At the bottom of the locks, the canal crosses over the River Goyt by the way of this splendid aqueduct, designed by Benjamin Outram, and built in 1795−99. It is 100 feet high and its construction was supervised by a local engineer, Thomas Brown. The design is said to be vaguely Roman in style, deliberately so as to enhance the view across the valley. The circular stone openings lessen the weight of the structure whilst keeping its strength. It is the tallest masonry arch aqueduct in the UK.

The aqueduct makes an interesting contrast with the adjoining railway viaduct, built in 1865, which took only one year to complete.

Right: Posset Bridge, Peak Forest Canal, Marple.

Below: Romiley canal aqueduct on the Peak Forest Canal.

Pear New Mill,
Bredbury.

Pear New Mill, Bredbury

Built in 1912, this mill building was to be the first phase of a larger project, but the second phase, to be called Apple Mill, was never built.

The mill comprises a five-storey structure built in red Accrington brick with a yellow-brick and terracotta decoration, with a two-storey carding extension on the west side. A separate engine house has art nouveau terracotta panels.

The most distinctive feature of the mill is the pear-shaped dome of the water tower at the south-east corner of the building, but there are also two smaller pear-shaped decorations at the western corners of the main roof.

The mill ceased to be used for textile purposes in 1966 and is now the Pear Industrial Estate. The main pear feature was provided with floodlighting a few years ago.

Peel Moat

This curious earthwork is a perfect square, its sides facing due north, south, east and west. It comprises a slightly raised central mound with sides 110 feet long surrounded by a moat, the outer sides of which are 220 feet long.

The origins of Peel Moat have long puzzled local historians. The name itself suggests a defensive purpose, and it may have been put to such use. Other suggestions include an association with local hunting, a protected site for animals, or a Roman survey marker.

The most convincing explanation was made by former Stockport Local History Librarian David Reid, who suggested that it was a Roman signal station associated with the fort at Castlefield.

Peel Moat,
Heaton Moor.

Perry, Fred

This tennis star of yesteryear was born in 1909 in Carrington Road, although his early years saw his family move to several locations in the north of England as his father was involved in local politics. By the age of eleven he was living in Ealing, West London.

After playing table tennis for a time, by the 1930s, he was playing in the Wimbledon tennis championships, winning the men's title three times, in 1934, 35 and 36. The

Birthplace of Fred Perry,
Carrington Road.

Fred Perry House.

final game was against Baron Gottfried von Cramm, which was over in less than forty-five minutes, establishing a record as the quickest final in the twentieth century and the second quickest ever. Perry also led the British Davis Cup team to victories over France, the USA and Australia in 1934–36.

He was always considered a bit of a working-class outsider in the corridors of Wimbledon, and the All England Members Club Tie, awarded to all Championship winners, was not formally presented to him, but left on a chair in his dressing room. In late 1936, he turned professional, which led to further ostracism within the British tennis establishment. As a result, he spent much of his later career playing abroad.

From the 1940s onwards, he became involved with creating a clothing brand, which exists to this day.

He has been called 'one of the six greatest players of all time'. In Stockport, Fred Perry House, housing Stockport Metropolitan Borough Council's headquarters, next to the Town Hall, was opened in 2010, and from 2002, the 14-mile Fred Perry Way footpath was created, running from Woodford to Reddish. He was made a Freeman of the Borough in 1934.

Plaza Theatre

Originally opened in October 1932, this art deco building was designed as for 'cine-variety' whereby live acts would be interspersed into film programmes. This was because it was felt that a more diversified use would guarantee the building's commercial viability. Consequently, the theatre has a suite of changing rooms around and underneath the stage area. After a few years, it became a normal cinema, although live shows continued to be put on from time to time. Total seating capacity was 1873. It was designed to be similar to the Regal Cinema, Altrincham, built by the same owners, the Snape Cinema circuit. The architect was Walter Thornley and its construction involved cutting 10,000 tons out of the sandstone rock face at the rear.

The building had a quite spectacular internal lighting system allowing different colours to be shown in sequence. A three-manual Compton theatre organ was also provided.

Its use as a cinema came to an end in December 1966 and it then became a Mecca bingo hall. A group of enthusiasts continued to maintain the organ, however, and recitals on it took place a couple of times a year.

Following closure as a bingo hall in 1999, a movement to secure the long-term preservation of this interesting building, now one of the few 'super cinemas' left in the country, started to grow, and a trust was established to acquire and restore it, aided by the local authority. The building reopened in December 2000 and in 2009 the theatre was closed to allow a £1.9M restoration scheme to proceed using Heritage Lottery Fund money. The interior now looks magnificent and the original lighting scheme has been restored, although some modifications, for example to allow greater accessibility, have also been carried out and the overall seating capacity is now reduced from the original. Further smaller-scale restoration works have been carried out subsequently. It has been used on a number of occasions as a filming location when a historic cinema environment is required.

A full programme of live shows, film screenings (some of which are 'vintage' film nights) and other events are put on. On the first floor, the old cinema café has itself been restored and is open for light meals.

The Plaza Theatre, Mersey Square.

The Queen's Head

The public house, on Little Underbank, is Stockport's oldest. Established in 1764, it was taken over by the Turner family in 1809 and for many years it was called Turner's Vaults, a name which is still occasionally used today.

It is currently named after Queen Anne, who reigned between 1702 and 1714.

There are three rooms comprising a narrow front bar complete with alcoves and a grandfather clock, a central 'snug' (which can seat only around six), and a quieter more comfortable room at the rear. The building was remodelled in 1930 and again in 1990.

The pub reputedly has the smallest toilet in Europe and a windowless 'haunted room'. A unique feature worth looking at are the two 'spirit cocks' on the top of the bar counter. Until 1935, these served spirits fed from the store in the wine merchants' premises above.

The Queen's Head, Little Underbank.

R

Reddish Mills and Sir William Houldsworth's Village

The suburb of Reddish, now heavily developed and industrialised, was still being described as 'predominantly agricultural' in 1857, although the Stockport Branch of the Ashton under Lyne Canal, which passed through Reddish, had been opened in 1797.

In the 1860s, Manchester-born Sir William Henry Houldsworth bought land adjoining the canal and from 1863 to 1865 built Reddish Mills, or Houldsworth Mill. At the time, this was claimed as the largest cotton-spinning mill in the world. It is, even today, an imposing building. A number of other mills were built in the area in the years that followed.

Houldsworth laid out a model village for his workers. Some of these houses still stand; others have succumbed to past slum clearance initiatives. The houses fronting the mill, on Houldsworth Street, are the most substantial and were intended for managerial and supervisory staff. Further away from the mill, the houses became more modest in size and quality. One of them, on David Street, has a blue plaque

Houldsworth Mill, Reddish, main elevation.

commemorating Joseph Lister VC (1886–1963) who lived here between 1939 and 1963. He served in the First Battalion of the Lancashire Fusiliers and gained his award for bravery in the Battle of Passchendaele in 1917.

Other facilities included a school, and an institute (now the Houldsworth Working Men's Club), built in 1874, and St Elisabeth's Church (see separate entry). The mill, village and institute were all designed by architect Abraham Stott.

Left: Better-class housing for supervisory staff on Houldsworth Street, Reddish.

Below: The Institute, now Working Men's Club, Leamington Road, Reddish.

Detail above the main entrance on Houldsworth Mill.

Houldsworth Square is in the present-day centre of Reddish. It includes a drinking fountain and four-sided clock, financed by public subscription, that dates from 1920, commemorating Houldsworth, who had died in 1917.

Houldsworth Mill ceased to be used for textile purposes in 1958. Following a recent £12M regeneration scheme by Stockport Council, it now houses a number of uses.

Reddish Vale

Reddish Vale is now home to a Country Park, comprising some 161 hectares including former mill lodges, a visitor centre and a butterfly park. The Trans Pennine Trail also passes through the park.

The vale was originally the home of a print works, founded in a small way in 1780 but substantially expanded during the nineteenth century. In 1899 it became one of the factories operated by the Calico Printers Association. During the Second World War, the factory was used to process Irish moss seaweed collected from the British coastline. Seaweed extract, carrageen, was dried to a flaky powder and used as a thickening agent in toothpaste, cosmetics, emulsion paints and printing colours. This replaced Japanese agar-agar, which was no longer available. The factory was still doing some of this work in the 1960s, when it was known locally as the 'Seaweed Factory'.

The works itself finally closed down in the early 1970s and the whole area was bought by a property company who proposed to develop a safari park on the surrounding land. Permission for this was refused and the land was then sold to the Greater Manchester Council. The old mill buildings had been turned into small industrial units. Post-1986, the site came into Stockport Council's ownership. Over the years, the old buildings were gradually cleared, eventually making way for the Butterfly Conservation Field, which opened in 1999.

Crossing the vale is Reddish Vale Railway Viaduct, built in 1875. It is claimed that a local witch put a curse on anyone who was willing to count the number of arches, so unhappy she was at the building of the line.

In March 1960, two Norwegian students from Manchester University, Eric Hof and Lars Ele, organised the building of a ski jump in the vale, to raise money for World Refugee Year. The ski jump was on the Denton side of the river and was constructed of scaffolding to a height of 40 feet. Snow was acquired partly from cold stores in Manchester and Liverpool and partly brought by road (and this in the pre-motorway age) – some 20 tons of it from the Devil's Elbow in Scotland. The snow had to be treated with carbon dioxide and the ground covered with ammonium chloride to prevent the snow from melting. It was spread around by volunteers with spades and the run ended in a grass bed.

Up to 15,000 watched the event, which started at 2.30 p.m. and was spread over two days. Admission for spectators was 2 shillings and 6 pence (12.5p). Over 100 British and Norwegian Olympic-standard skiers took part, making jumps of over 100 feet. A programme was printed, television and national newspapers gave it coverage, the St John Ambulance and the police were in attendance and a wind band provided music.

It was a great public event and is still remembered today with affection by those who were there. Thankfully some of it was captured on cine film, which can be seen today, courtesy of YouTube.

The main mill reservoir, Reddish Vale.

The former Reform Club.

Reform Club

The building, located on Wellington Street, dates from 1889 and was used by the Liberal Party. The architects were Manchester-based J. W. Beaumont & Sons, who had also designed the city's Whitworth Institute, now the Whitworth Art Gallery.

The Stockport Reform Club became a nightclub in 1975, sometimes called 'Cobdens', and in 2014 it was converted into stylish apartments and renamed Joseph Leigh House.

Robinsons Brewery

Officially the Unicorn Brewery, this is located on a very tight site just off Lower Hillgate, where the original Unicorn Inn once stood, first bought by William Robinson in 1838. The first Robinsons' Ale was brewed there in 1849 by his son, George.

Expansion followed from 1859, when Frederick took over, and from 1878 to 1890 the family acquired twelve public houses, starting what was to become an estate of more than 300 pubs located in north-west England, with a few in north Wales, many of which remain in company ownership today.

Robinsons Brewery, main entrance.

The brewery remains family-owned, and because of its relatively small scale, it has managed to avoid the forced divestment of public house estates that have obliged many of the larger breweries to create separately owned 'pubcos'. Over the years it has taken over other breweries. At a site in nearby Bredbury, the company provides casking, kegging and bottling services to other breweries.

The brewery remains one of a few to retain production by tower. A visitor centre, accessed via Apsley Street, was opened a few years ago and is well worth visiting. Do have a try at their 'Old Tom' beer; it certainly packs a punch!

Roman Bridge

This ancient packhorse bridge, between Marple and New Mills, is not Roman at all. The adjective 'Roman' was added to it in the 1700s when the area became popular with tourists.

Roman Bridge, between Marple and Strines.

Roman Lakes

Samuel Oldknow's great Mellor Mill was destroyed by fire in 1892 and was not rebuilt. Since the coming of the railway to Marple in 1865, the area had become increasingly popular with weekend tourists keen to enjoy the countryside in the area.

The Furniss family, one of whom, Edwin, had been the last manager of the mill, in 1892 set up the Roman Lakes Company Ltd based around the old mill reservoirs, first leasing then purchasing the lands from the Arkwrights, the last owners of the mill. There was never any true Roman connection; it was just felt that describing the lakes as 'Roman' would enhance their attractiveness to visitors. The Marple band played every Sunday, dancing took place, boats could be hired on the lake and slot machines made an appearance. In winter, if conditions were right, ice skating could take place. Thousands would descend on Marple in the 1920s and 1930s to enjoy the pleasures provided by the Roman Lakes.

Since then, the slot machines, bands and dancing have gone as boating was found to conflict with the needs of the angling community, among whom the lakes are very popular.

One of the Roman Lakes.

S

Scotch 'Bob' Cheadle

This wooden carving commemorates 'Scotch Bob', or James Telford, who was associated with the provision of public transport in Cheadle for many years.

Originating from Dumfriesshire, Scotch Bob came to Cheadle in 1871. By 1879 he was employed by the Manchester Carriage Company driving their red horse-drawn buses. By 1908 he had set a British record by driving over 60,000 miles on the Cheadle to Manchester route. When driving he would frequently quote his fellow countryman Robbie Burns and he knew everyone along the routes he travelled. He would raise his whip in greeting, even when it was raining heavily.

In 1913, his job changed to that of timekeeper at the White Hart terminus, after motor buses had been introduced. He lived on Gatley Road, close to the White Hart. He died in 1929.

'Scotch Bob' statue, Cheadle.

This carving was done by Andy Burgess, being created from an oak trunk some 3.5 metres high and 1 metre wide. The work took four days to complete and was done using a variety of chainsaws and other power tools.

Staircase Café

This building is another of Stockport's most historic buildings, and has been the subject of considerable local effort to secure its preservation.

The shop itself is built around a fifteenth-century cruck frame, whilst the cellar shows signs of medieval origin. Rising from the rear of the building, for its full height, is an intricately carved early seventeenth-century staircase, which gave the former café its name. The staircase is said to be of a rare type for the North West, and is described as a caged newel staircase, in which the four inner newel posts rise the full height of the building without interruption.

Many of the upper-floor rooms have seventeenth- and eighteenth-century oak panelling, of high quality suggesting that the building was of some local significance, such as the town house of a notable county family.

Unfortunately, fires in November 1989 and the mid-1990s damaged some seventeenth-century areas at the rear of the property, and parts of the roof. In the mid-

Staircase House, Market Place.

1990s, the property was bought by the local authority, and a bid, ultimately successful, was made for National Lottery funding for a full restoration scheme, which has now been completed. The building now contains the town's tourist information centre, and the 'Stockport Story' display formerly located in the town's Vernon Park Museum.

Stockport Grammar School

Stockport Grammar School is the second oldest school of secular foundation in the UK, being founded under the will of London merchant and one-time Lord Mayor Sir Edmund Shaa in 1487.

Originally founded in the town's parish church, it moved to its own separate site on Chestergate, given by Stockport mayor Alexander Lowe, in 1607, where it remained until 1832. It then moved to a larger site on Wellington Road South, roughly where the Art Gallery and part of the present Stockport College site are now located, where it remained until 1915. It then moved to its present site on Buxton Road. In 1979 it took over the adjoining Convent High School site, when it became co-educational, and its subsequent history has been one of continuous development and improvement.

The Grammar School has consistently achieved high educational standards, sending many of its pupils on to Oxbridge and into public life. In the early years of schools 'league tables', in one year it was placed as the highest co-educational school in England. The school runs a 'house' system of four houses, named after prominent Stockport families of the past, namely Arden, Nicholson, Vernon and Warren. Its school magazine, *The Stopfordian*, is one of the longest-running school magazines in the UK. Past pupils are referred to as 'Old Stopfordians' or 'Old Stops' as opposed to 'Stopfordians', which denotes an inhabitant of the current borough.

Stockport Grammar School, main entrance.

Above left: Plaque on Chestergate indicating the school's second location.

Above right: Plaque on Wellington Road South near the Art Gallery marking the school's third location.

Small metal plaques mark the sites of the school's second and third locations.

Almost opposite, on the other side of Buxton Road, is Stockport School, previously a local authority-run state grammar school.

Stockport Parish Church

Sometimes known as 'St Marys in the Marketplace', this is the oldest surviving building in Stockport. The chancel dates from before 1334.

St Mary's was the place where Stockport Grammar School was founded in 1487. In 1602, Judge John Bradshaw, who sentenced Charles I to death, was baptised here.

The church's original tower was cracked by the continuous ringing of the bells in celebration of the British victory at Trafalgar, so much so that both nave and bell tower had to be rebuilt in 1814.

The church is a Grade I listed building and in the early 2000s was subject to much restoration work and the provision of additional toilets and a kitchen. It shares, with St George's Church, Great Moor, the role of being Stockport's 'civic church', although St George's is larger. In 2000, Stockport Heritage Trust opened a small Heritage Centre inside the building.

Stockport Parish Church in the Market Place.

St Thomas's, Higher Hillgate

This neoclassical church was built between 1822 and 1825. It is what is known as a 'Waterloo Church' or a 'Commissioners Church' as it was built to both celebrate Wellington's victory over Napoleon at Waterloo in 1815, but also as an unemployment relief project with the aim of reducing the chances of revolution among the working classes.

The church cost £15,611 and the whole cost was covered by a grant from the Church Building Commission. The land for it was donated by Lady Warren-Bulkeley.

Initial seating for 2,000 was provided, and the church has a splendid gallery on three sides, now alas out of use. Refurbishments and remodelling took place in 1881 and 1890, and some work has been done more recently. It is Grade I listed.

The church has a rectangular shape and is built of sandstone. There is a clock tower at the western end and a portico with six Ionic columns at the eastern end. The overall design was by George Basevi.

A three-manual organ was provided in 1834 by Samuel Renn, somewhat altered since.

St Thomas's Church, Higher Hillgate.

Strawberry Studios

Located on Waterloo Road, the studio facilities at this site ran from 1968 to 1993 and it was the place where many famous bands made recordings.

Originally located in a music store in the town centre, and called 'Inter-City Studios', the building was bought in 1968 by Peter Tattersall, a former road manager for Billy J. Kramer and the Dakotas. He then invited Eric Stewart, later to be a member of 10cc, to join him in the new venture. Stewart chose the new name for the venue after his favourite Beatles song 'Strawberry Fields Forever'.

Graham Gouldman soon joined the partnership and the studio was used by 10cc (from 1977) and by other artists such as The Smiths, The Stone Roses, Neil Sedaka, The Syd Lawrence Orchestra, Paul McCartney and Cliff Richard.

Studio equipment was continuously improved over the years, and at times it was operating on a twenty-four-hour basis. Many memorable recordings were made there.

10cc sold their interest in Strawberry Studios in the early 1980s, and in 1986 its operation was taken over by the neighbouring Yellow Two studios. Following a period of being used for video and film recording, it finally ceased operation in 1993 and the building is now used as offices, although it retains the Strawberry Studios title and an appropriate blue plaque.

In 2017, Stockport Museum ran an exhibition about the studios, including recreating its control panel. It proved popular and was extended twice.

Above: Strawberry Studios.

Left: Commemorative plaque at Strawberry Studios.

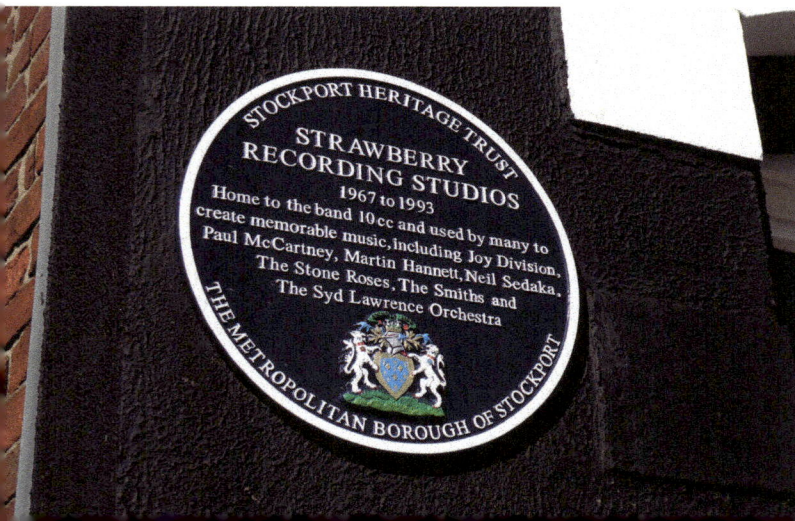

Town Hall

Stockport's Town Hall, locally described as 'The Wedding Cake', was built in 1904–08 to a design by Sir Alfred Bramwell Thomas, who had also designed Belfast City Hall. It was formally opened by the Prince and Princess of Wales and to mark the event, one of the town's main shopping streets, Heaton Lane, had part of it renamed as Princes Street, a name it retains today.

When the building was first erected, it was not possible to include bells in the main clock tower, as it was feared that these would disturb patients in the former Stockport Infirmary, located in a notable neoclassical building on the opposite side of the A6.

Three oak-panelled committee rooms were provided along with a Council Chamber, which contains elaborate plasterwork, brass chandeliers and decorative oak benches. Nearby are some interesting male toilets (only men were councillors and aldermen in those days!).

Adjoining is a ballroom, built at the same time. John Betjeman described this as 'magnificent'. It contains a Wurlitzer organ, formerly located at Manchester's Paramount – later Odeon Theatre – subsequently moved to the Free Trade Hall in 1977, and since 1999, located here, courtesy of the Lancastrian Theatre Organ Trust.

A decorative coloured floodlighting scheme was provided to the main frontage recently.

Stockport Town Hall.

Underbank Hall

This building, more commonly known as Great Underbank Hall, is said to be Stockport's most historic house. Its exact age is unknown, but it is thought to date from the late fifteenth or early sixteenth centuries.

It was the town house of one of Stockport's most influential families, the Arderns of Bredbury, who owned it until 1823, when it was sold at auction. At the time of the sale attempts were made to turn the building into a town hall for Stockport, but it was bought by a syndicate comprising W. Miller Christie, Isaac Lloyd, John Worsley and J. K. Winterbottom, who formed the Stockport and Cheshire Bank.

It was first used as a bank in 1829, and became one of the first branches of the District Bank Ltd, which itself became part of the NatWest Group in 1968.

The front of the hall contains original oak-panelled rooms, with 'eight-light' windows that run almost continuously along the lower storey. The rear is a large banking hall, built in 1915, containing a magnificent seventeenth-century fireplace originally from Uppingham Hall. Over the fireplace is a plaque commemorating the initial founders of the bank, and a list of the branch managers from 1929 to the present day. The branch manager's office contains a similar fireplace.

The whole building remains in use as a bank and it is sympathetically maintained by NatWest.

Underbank Hall, Great Underbank in the town centre.

V

Vernon Park and Museum

Ten acres of land, known as 'Stringer's Fields', were donated by Lord Vernon (George John Warren) to Stockport Corporation in 1842 for provision of a public park. A further 11 acres were retained by Lord Vernon, to be used for building, but he later sold it to a local surgeon, who in 1851 resold it to the council for the same price, making the total site just over 21 acres.

Work finally started on laying out the new park in November 1857, and it opened to the public on 20 September 1858. Lying on the banks of the River Goyt, it was originally called The People's Park or Pinch Belly Park. It is Stockport's oldest park.

The park is a particularly good example of a Victorian and Edwardian public park, with ponds, statues, a fountain, rock work and areas of woodland adjoining the river. It holds Grade II status in the Historic England Register of Historic Parks and Gardens. There are a number of glacial 'erratics' or boulders strewn around the park. The one near to the museum entrance is the largest, weighing over 2.5 tons, and was found under Coronation Street, Edgeley, in 1886.

A substantial grant from the Heritage Lottery Fund led to a very good restoration of its original features, completed in September 2000.

General view of Vernon Park.

Vernon Park museum building.

The museum opened in October 1860 and was the gift of the town's two Members of Parliament, James Kershaw and John Benjamin Smith, whose generosity is commemorated in a plaque on the front of the building. Originally, the building had its museum on the ground floor and an art gallery on the first floor. A new wing was added in 1866.

Following the opening of 'The Stockport Story' in the town centre, the use of the museum building has gradually changed. Much of the ground floor is a café, art displays take place in the basement and the upper floor is used as meeting rooms. At the foot of the stairs leading to the first floor is the 'Blue John Window', created by the museum's first curator, John Tym, who originated from Castleton, where 'Blue John' is mined. The window is made up of thin strips of the blue translucent rock.

Viaduct

Dominating the town centre, the railway viaduct has been claimed to be the largest brick-built engineering structure in the UK. Originally built for the Manchester and Birmingham Railway between March and December 1839, it first comprised some 400 cubic feet of stonework and around 11 million bricks. One writer, in 1842, stated

Stockport Viaduct, southwards view.

that the bricks used, if laid end to end, would exceed the whole length of the Great Wall of China.

The viaduct was doubled in width in 1888–89. The total length is 1,780 feet, with twenty-six arches, of which twenty-two have a span of 63 feet each. The height of the parapet is 111 feet above the River Mersey.

In the late 1980s, the structure was cleaned and provided with floodlighting in a scheme carried out by British Rail and the local authority.

W

War Memorial Art Gallery

The idea of creating a memorial to the fallen of the First World War was first mooted in 1919. Three ideas were considered: for a monument, an art gallery and a memorial hall. The matter was resolved when the trustees of the late Samuel Kay gave the site with the stipulation that the memorial building should contain an art gallery. A temporary memorial was erected on the site in 1921.

On 15 September 1923, the foundation stone was laid by the Mayor, Alderman Charles Royle. It contains the inscription 'In memory of the men of Stockport who fell in the Great War (1914–1918)'.

War Memorial Art Gallery, main entrance on Wellington Road South.

Art Gallery,
interior view.

The building was designed by Theodore Halliday and built by local contractors Daniel Eadie & Co. It was finished in 1925 and formally opened on 15 October by Prince Henry. Designed to complement the nearby Town Hall, it is a neoclassical revival building fronted by a grand portico with four Corinthian columns. The overall design is said to be loosely based on the temple of Apollo at Bassae.

Inside, on either side, are exhibition rooms, with the main gallery area upstairs. At the rear is the Hall of Memory, which contains the names of more than 2,200 of the fallen. There are more Corinthian columns here, much marble and the entire hall is lit by four corner bronze pedestal lamps. In the centre of the hall at the front is an impressive sculpture group comprising life-sized figures of Britannia and a man. The whole Hall of Memory is surprisingly effective and moving.

Whalley, Joanne

Although not born in Stockport, actress Joanne Whalley was brought up in the borough, attending schools in Bredbury, Harrytown Convent (see separate entry) and a speech and drama school in Marple.

Her first acting roles were as a child in shows like *Juliet Bravo*, and also playing bit-parts in various soap operas. A short spell in the music industry followed, in groups such as the Stockport-based Slowguns, and later Cindy and the Saffrons.

In 1982, at the age of twenty-one, her first big break came through Granada Television's production of Stan Barstow's *A Kind of Loving*. Subsequent television appearances included *The Singing Detective* and *The Good Father* (1985).

Joanne Whalley at the Cannes Film Festival to promote her film *Breathtaking*, 12 May 2000. (Paul Smith/ Featureflash photo agency/Shutterstock)

She married Val Kilmer in 1988 and subsequently moved to Los Angeles, and became well-known in Hollywood, starring in many films. In 1989 she played the role of Christine Keeler In *Scandal*, which dealt with the 1960s Profumo affair. From her marriage until 1996, she was known professionally as Joanne Whalley-Kilmer.

Subsequent roles have included playing Jacqueline Kennedy, Queen Mary I, the mistress of a Cardinal and the wife of Pontius Pilate. Her screen and stage career continues.

Whitworth, Sir Joseph

Whitworth was born in 1803 on John Street, near the centre of the town. He was educated at Idle, West Yorkshire, and later was apprenticed to his uncle, Joseph Hulse, who ran a cotton-spinning mill at Oakerthorpe in Derbyshire. During this time, he began to develop a keen interest in mechanics, in particular being interested in the poor quality and accuracy of the milling machinery then in use, which he resolved to address.

Subsequent career moves saw him developing precision machine tools and he helped with the development of the Difference Machine, Charles Babbage's calculating machine, an early mechanical computer. In 1833, he founded his own company, manufacturing lathes and other tools. Twenty years later, along with his friend George Wallis, he was appointed a British Commissioner for the New York

International Exhibition. His career also saw him involved with the development of the Whitworth Rifle and breech-loading artillery.

'The Firs', a grand house in Fallowfield, Manchester, was built for him in 1850 by the architect Edward Walters. It is currently used as a hotel and conference centre by the University of Manchester. In 1872, Whitworth and his family moved to Stancliffe Hall in Darley Dale, Derbyshire.

By 1850, he was a president of the Institution of Mechanical Engineers and in 1859 became an honorary member of the Institution of Engineers and Shipbuilders in Scotland. The year 1857 saw him being elected a Fellow of the Royal Society.

He supported the founding of Manchester's Mechanics Institution and the Manchester School of Design. In 1868 he founded the Whitworth Scholarship, which aimed to bring science and industry closer together, and which still exists today. Some ten to fifteen scholarships are awarded each year.

He died in 1887, leaving a substantial sum to be devoted to philanthropic projects. One of his will's legatees was Richard Christie. The legatees spent their money on projects which Whitworth himself would have supported, so the Christie Hospital, Whitworth Hall (part of the University), Whitworth Park and Art Gallery all benefited in this way. His name appears many times in Manchester, including Whitworth Street in the city centre.

Williams, Fred

The stories of Alan Turing and Tommy Flowers in the development of computing have been told many times. The former laid the foundations of modern computer science and built the first mechanical computer, while the latter built the first electronic machine. Both were at Bletchley Park during the Second World War.

The Manchester area played its part also – it was the place where the first stored programme computer was built and it was a Stockport-born man, Fred Williams, who was heavily involved in it.

Sir Frederic Calland Williams, or 'Freddie' or just 'FC', was born in Romiley in 1911. Educated at Stockport Grammar School and Manchester University, his early work saw him at the large Metropolitan Vickers factory in Trafford Park, but this was soon interrupted to do research work at Oxford, where in 1936 he gained a DPhil. He returned to work at Manchester University. In 1939 he was invited to join the radar research establishment at Bawdsey in East Anglia. His research work continued unabated during the war years.

Shortly after the war he visited the USA on a number of occasions where he came across ENIAC, the first general purpose electronic computer, but still without a stored programme capability. On his return to the UK, he turned his attention to the possibility of using cathode ray tubes for storage purposes. The 'Williams Tube', or more correctly the 'Williams-Kilburn Tube', after Tom Kilburn his colleague, proved to be the answer.

Fred Williams' birthplace, Romiley.

In June 1948, the Small Scale Experimental Machine, or 'Baby', ran at Manchester University. The first task of this quite large machine was a simple square root calculation. The world has not looked back since.

Williams continued work on early computers, including the Manchester Mark 1, though his later work was in the field of electrical engineering. He formally opened a new science block at his old school, Stockport Grammar, in the late 1950s. He was knighted in 1976 and died the following year.

A few years ago, a reconstruction of 'Baby' was built at the Greater Manchester Museum of Science and Industry.

Wilson, Charlie

Wilson was an English footballer who played for both Stockport County and Liverpool football clubs. He was born in Stockport in 1877 (though another source states that he came from Shropshire).

Whilst with Liverpool, the club won the League title in 1901.

He retired in 1905 following a broken leg on the field, which he had predicted in a dream, but continued working for Liverpool in a scouting and training role until 1939.

Winters Clockhouse

This shop was originally established as a jewellers in 1859 and in around 1880 it was taken over by Jacob Winter. Prominent on the frontage are three painted figures (Father Time, a Victorian guardsman and a sailor), which struck the bells above every fifteen minutes.

The left-hand shop window featured a unique hydraulically operated security device which lowered the entire window display into the shop cellar at the end of each day. Additional security was also offered by the fact that, like its neighbours, the shop was built into the sandstone rock face and has no rear exit.

The shop closed down because of declining trade in 1988 and the clock was later damaged by a passing vehicle, but in 1991–92 it was restored and reopened as a wine bar and restaurant, called appropriately 'Winter's', and its clock mechanism could be seen in working order by patrons. At the time of writing it was closed.

Winter's Clockhouse.

Wood, Wilfred

Wilfred Wood was born in February 1897 in Hazel Grove. He served with the Northumberland Fusiliers in the First World War and in 1918 was serving in Italy fighting the forces of the Austro-Hungarian empire.

For conspicuous bravery and initiative on 28 October 1918 near Casa Van, during which he single-handedly brought about the surrender of over 300 enemy troops, he was awarded the Victoria Cross.

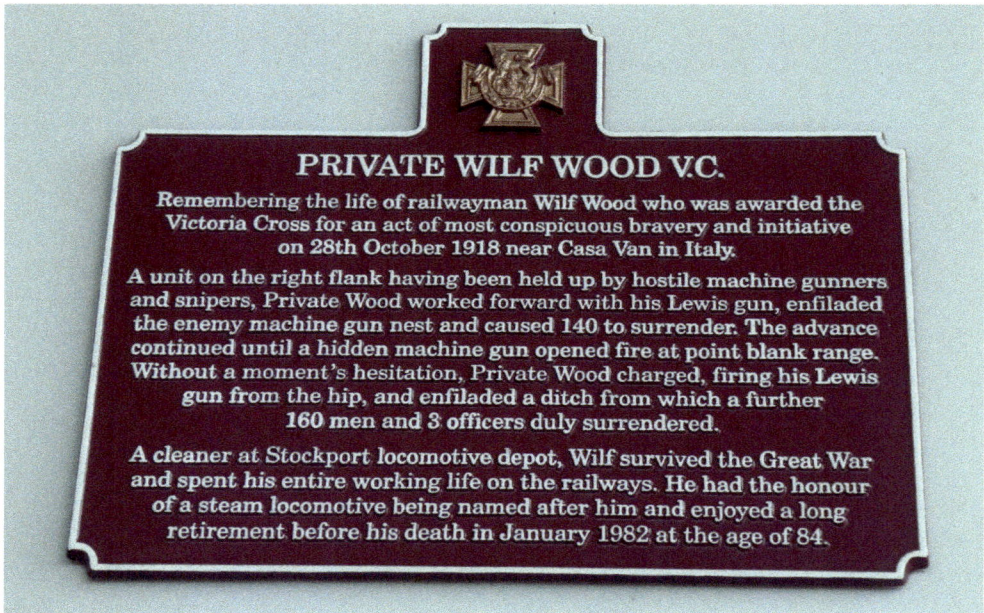

PRIVATE WILF WOOD V.C.

Remembering the life of railwayman Wilf Wood who was awarded the Victoria Cross for an act of most conspicuous bravery and initiative on 28th October 1918 near Casa Van in Italy.

A unit on the right flank having been held up by hostile machine gunners and snipers, Private Wood worked forward with his Lewis gun, enfiladed the enemy machine gun nest and caused 140 to surrender. The advance continued until a hidden machine gun opened fire at point blank range. Without a moment's hesitation, Private Wood charged, firing his Lewis gun from the hip, and enfiladed a ditch from which a further 160 men and 3 officers duly surrendered.

A cleaner at Stockport locomotive depot, Wilf survived the Great War and spent his entire working life on the railways. He had the honour of a steam locomotive being named after him and enjoyed a long retirement before his death in January 1982 at the age of 84.

Above: Plaque at Stockport Station commemorating Wilfred Wood.

Left: Sign at the Wilfred Wood public house, Hazel Grove.

After the war he returned to working on the railways as a cleaner at Edgeley locomotive depot. A Claughton-class locomotive was named after him in 1922 by the London and North Western Railway Company; later a Patriot-class locomotive was given the same name by the London Midland and Scottish Railway. This nameplate resided in a primary school in Hazel Grove for many years, and is now located in the Fusiliers Museum of Northumberland at Alnwick Castle.

He died in January 1982 at the age of eighty-four. A Wetherspoons public house named after him was opened in Hazel Grove in 2010 and this plaque is on display in the ticket foyer of Stockport Station.

Wybersley Hall, High Lane

Sometimes spelt Wyberslegh Hall, this house is where the author Christopher Isherwood was born. It was formerly in the ownership of the Bradshaw family, one of whom, John, born 1602, signed the death warrant for Charles I in 1649.

The building dates from various times, the earliest of which is the fifteenth century. It became a listed building in 1967. The front of the building has castellations on both gable wing and the central wall that connects them. It is a private residence and close access is not possible.

Wybersley Hall, High Lane.

X

Plant, Elsie and Suffragette Square

Well 'X' was always going to be a difficult letter to fill, but allow me to use 'X' on the ballot paper – at least as far as women getting the right to vote is concerned – as a way of solving this issue.

Although born in Calderdale, Elsie Plant spent most of her life living in Stockport, and is one of the town's contributions to the suffragette movement.

She was born in 1890. After campaigning for women's suffrage, she and her husband Walter became actively involved in the Labour Party in Stockport. She also became involved in promoting birth control and attempted to open a clinic in 1923 in the town. This was defeated following opposition from the Roman Catholic Church.

She also became friends with Marie Stopes and arranged for her to address an audience of over 2,000 on the subject at the Armoury.

Her philosophy in life was that of defending the rights of women to self-determination.

In March 2018, the new square between Princes Street and the new Redrock development was named 'Suffragette Square' after Elsie Plant, Gertrude Powicke (suffragist and the only woman to be named on a First World War memorial in the town), Elizabeth Raffald (eighteenth-century benefactor, cookery writer and businesswoman) and Hannah Winbolt (silk weaver and suffragette).

Suffragette Square, off St Petersgate.

Y

Yarwood, Mike

In these days of multi-channel television, cable and streaming services, large audiences are becoming harder to achieve for broadcast television stations. Many look back to the days of Christmas 1977 when comedians Morecambe and Wise attracted an audience of nearly 21.3 million viewers (often erroneously quoted as 28 million) to their Christmas special show.

The accolade of the highest number of viewers to any television show actually goes to the show that preceded it on the night, featuring Bredbury-born Mike Yarwood, whose show slightly topped that at 21.4 million viewers.

Born in June 1941, Yarwood's television career started in 1964 when he appeared on *Sunday Night at the London Palladium.* He appeared on both ITV and the BBC.

His stock in trade was impersonations of political figures of the day, his most memorable being Labour Prime Minister Harold Wilson. Other politicians were also caricatured, along with sports commentators, political journalists, football managers, etc.

With the advent of a Conservative government in 1979, his career began to go into decline, as many of his stock characters disappeared from our screens and he was unable to master their replacements. Thames TV cancelled his show at the end of 1987 and he has not appeared regularly since.

Zurich Gardens, Bramhall

This pleasant little cul-de-sac on the edges of Bramhall merits the entry under the letter 'Z' in this book. It is located on an estate with other roads named after places in Switzerland, such as Lugano Road, Lucerne Road, etc.

Zurich Gardens has also the distinction of being the last alphabetical street name in the United Kingdom, unless the names of individual apartment blocks are counted, in which case Zyburn Court in not-that-far-away Salford would take the prize!

Zurich Gardens, Bramhall.

Acknowledgements

Books of this nature can only be written with the willing assistance of a great many people. Thanks are due to the many employees and volunteers at heritage attractions, including the area's churches, who have granted me access, allowed me to take photographs and patiently answered my questions.

Much information for this book, has been garnered from visits over the years to the area's excellent public libraries and archive departments. The pages of other books, guidebooks, the internet, tourist and publicity material produced have also been useful sources of information, and acknowledgements are due to the various authors who have provided material for adaptation in the book. Particular acknowledgements are due to the Stockport Heritage Trust, who have produced much work on the town and who continue to champion its heritage.

About the Author

Robert Nicholls has lived in the North West since 1973, holding various professional positions in local government and subsequently with Manchester Airports Group. Born in 1952 in Sheffield, he was educated at High Storrs Grammar School, has a degree in Estate Management from Reading University and is qualified as a chartered surveyor. In 2000, he gained an MBA from Lancaster University and in 2014, he was awarded, with distinction, the Advanced Diploma in Local History by Oxford University.

He retired in 2013, having served twenty-five years with the Manchester Airports Group, latterly as Regulation Manager.

He is interested in local and transport history with particular emphasis on related economic development and land use changes. His previous publications include *Manchester's Narrow Gauge Railways* (1985), *Looking Back at Belle Vue* (1989), *Heyhead Church 1862-1992* (1992), *The Belle Vue Story* (1992), *Trafford Park, the First 100 years* (1996), *Curiosities of Greater Manchester* (2004), *Haveley Hey School – Seventy Years of Service to the Community* (2005), *Curiosities of Merseyside* (2005), *The Church of the Ascension – a History 1970 – 2006* (2006), *St Chad's Church, Ladybarn – the story of a church and its people* (2007), *Curiosities of Cheshire* (2010), *Davyhulme Sewage Works and its Railway* (2015), *50 Gems of Staffordshire* (2017), *Secret Stafford* (2018), *50 Gems of Lancashire* (2019) and *A Legacy of love – the Harrison organ at St Chad's Church, Ladybarn* (2019). Kindle publications have included *Staffordshire Curiosities, Curiosities of the High Peak* and *The Curious Places of Lancashire*.

As well as contributing articles to magazines, he gives talks to local history societies.